The ABCs
Healthcare

A Journey Through Health and Healing

By Shakeema Funchess

This Book Belongs To:

_____

This book is dedicated to healthcare workers who

In times of sickness, pain, and fear,

You wipe away each trembling tear,

With kindness and compassion, you're the key,

For you make the world a better place to be

Bringing joy and warmth in countless ways

For you brighten our most challenging days!

Doctors and nurses, you lead the way,

With hearts of gold, come what may,

Patient access and support, a trusted band,

Together you lend a healing hand.

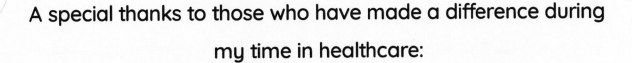

A special thanks to those who have made a difference during my time in healthcare:

Dr. Manjunath, ANM Pell, Nurse Stevens, Nurse Cebel, PA Manager Rodriguez, PA Manager Gardner, PA Supervisor Mclean, PA Specialist Powell, PA Specialist Hollner, PA Supervisor McGuire, PA Specialist Bueford, PA FC Specialist Acevedo, PA Specialist Baker, Nurse Brooks, Nurse Umayam, Dr. Pinto, Dr. Boyd Smith, Nurse Shuri, Tech Sweener, PA Rep Martinez, ANM Ebitz, Nurse Hanna, Nurse Rhodes, Epic Trainer Kolysko, Nurse Nicsevic, ANM Kircher, Nurse Hamlett, Nurse Ballard, Nurse Jeancharles, Nurse Yates, Nurse Liddie, IS System Manager Terplak, Tech Support Hubert, Dr. Telitsky, PA Specialist Akujuo, Nurse Patterson, PA Specialist Lumpkin, PA Specialist Green, PA Specialist Leonhardt, PA Specialist Macron, PA Specialist Coffey, PA AVP Pallozzi, PA Director Pascarella, PA Assoc Director Palmer, PA Admin Roth, PA Supervisor Garrow, Q &D Trainer Shaver, PA Specialist Henderer, PA Specialist Calvagno, PA Specialist Gross, PA

Specialist Latant, PA Specialist John, PA Specialist Addo, PA Specialist Sukhnandan, Dr. Pauze, Dr. Noonan, Dr. Chow, Dr. Asher, Dr. Cadigan, Dr. Cordi, Dr. Dailey, Dr. Donovan, Dr. Duncan, Dr. Furlano, Dr. Gillespie, Dr. Grajny, Dr. Hanowitz, Dr. Hogan, Dr. Long, Dr. Malabanan, Dr. Mckenna, Dr. Morrissey, Dr. Rowden, Dr. Snyder, Dr. Thevenin, Dr. Thibodeau, Dr. Tudor, Dr. Waldrop, Dr. Benson, Dr. Gunn, Dr. Lord, Dr. Lee, Dr. Potenza, Dr. Bringley, Dr. Shkolnik, PA Specialist Frederick, PA Specialist Gumbs, PA Specialist Thomas, PA Specialist Hughes, PA Coordinator Houston, PA Specialist Best, PA Specialist Bindner, PA Specialist Degan, PA Specialist LaFortune, PA Specialist Dickson, PA Specialist Thompson, PA Specialist Phelps, Liaison Ryals, Liaison Spielman, Liaison Shoaib, eMPI coordinator Files, eMPI App Specialist Trainor, Nurse Rosato, Nurse Clarkson, ANM Piusz, Patient Flow Specialist Young, Nurse Supervisor Kowalik, Epic Analyst Ballato, EVS Manager Maderic and so many more.

In the world of healthcare, for kids, you see,
There's an "ABC" guide, just for you and me.
From A to Z, let's explore and uncover,
The experts and tools that help kids recover.

A is for "Anesthesiologist," who helps kids sleep,
During surgery, their watch they keep.

B is for "Band-Aid," a small piece of aid,
To cover up boo-boos, so smiles aren't delayed.

C is for "Child Life Specialist," with toys and play,
They ease young minds during the hospital stay.

D is for "Dentist," who keeps teeth so bright,
Brushing and flossing to prevent any fright.

E is for "Emergency Room," when things get severe,
Doctors and nurses are there, have no fear.

F is for "Flu Shot," to keep illness at bay,
Vaccines helps kids stay healthy each day.

G is for "Gynecologist," for girls as they grow, Caring for their reproductive health, helping them to know.

is for "Hospitalist," who cares day and night.
In the hospital, they are a guiding light.

is for "Immunologist," exploring what's in store,
With allergies and immunity, they help kids even more.

J is for "Juvenile Rheumatologist," a specialist so keen,
They treat kids with joint and autoimmune issues unseen.

K is for "Kinesiologist," who studies movement so well.
Rehabilitation for kids, so their bodies do not swell.

is for "Laboratory Technician," in white coats,
Testing and analyzing, they take many notes.

M is for "Midwife," with expertise so wide,
Guiding mothers and newborns, on this joyful ride.

N is for "Nutritionist," guiding kids on what to eat. To keep them healthy and strong, from their heads to their feet.

is for "Optometrist," who checks kids' eyesight so clear,
Prescribing glasses or contacts, ensuring vision's near.

P is for "Patient Access," a crucial role, you see,
They help kids navigate healthcare registration,
making it easy as can be.

is for "Quarantine Specialist," who keeps infections at bay, Isolating sick children to prevent germs from spreading away.

R is for "Respiratory Therapist," who assists with every breath,
Helping kids with lung conditions, preventing health
problems in early steps.

S is for "Speech-Language Pathologist," with skills so fine, They help kids communicate, making words align.

is for "Therapist," who helps kids express
Their thoughts and their feelings to reduce their stress.

U is for "Ultrasound," for babies in the womb,
To check their development and see them soon.

is for "Vaccine," a shield against disease,
Protecting children's health with incredible ease.

is for "Wheelchair Specialist," who ensures the right fit,
Giving mobility to children, never letting them quit.

is for "X-ray Technician," with images they glean,
To see what's beneath, the unseen.

is for "Yoga," a calming technique,
To help kids relax when they feel weak.

Z is for "Zootherapy Specialist," who uses animals so dear,
To provide emotional support, bringing comfort and cheer.

From A to Z, the world of healthcare unfolds,
For children, the story of health never gets old.
With love and support, and professionals who care,
Kids thrive and grow, no matter what's in the air.

The End

Printed in the USA
CPSIA information can be obtained
at www.ICGtesting.com
LVRC091749131123
763809LV00002B/4